The Korean War Ex

Pocket

George Joshua

Published by G-L-R (Great Little Read)

Copyright: G-L-R

This book is sold subject to the condition that it shall not by way of trade or otherwise be resold or hired out or otherwise circulated without the written or verbal consent of the author

Written by George Joshua

Reading age for this book: 10+

Reading Age for the series will vary but usually starts at ten

Most books in this series have been written for children aged ten and over. It is the perfect tool for parents to get their children into the habit of reading.

This book has been created to entertain and educate young minds and is packed with information and trivia and lots of authentic images that bring the topic alive.

TABLE OF CONTENTS

An Introduction to the Korean War 6

Timeline 1 8

Japanese Control of Korea 9

The Start of the Korean War 11

Timeline 2 14

The Pusan Perimeter 15

UN Forces Attack North Korea 17

Timeline 3 19

The Chinese Attack South Korea 20

General Douglas MacArthur 24

The First Battle of Seoul 26

The Battle of Osan 28

The Battle of Inchon (Incheon) 30

The Second Battle of Seoul 32

The Battle of Ch'ongch'on River 35

The Battle of Chosin Reservoir 37

The Third Battle of Seoul 39

Operation Ripper 41

The Battle of Imjin River..43

Peace Talks 45

Korean War Trivia..47

Pocket History 49

Attributions...51

An Introduction to the Korean War

The Korean War was a conflict between North Korea and South Korea and was part of an overall Cold War between the Soviet Union and the USA (The Western Powers).

The Korean Peninsula before the Second World War had been part of Japan. When Japan was defeated, the peninsula was divided between the victorious allies.

The Soviet Union claimed the land to the north of the Peninsula, and the USA took control of the south.

The two parts of the peninsular were divided along the 38th Parallel, and it didn't take long for North and South Korea to form governments.

North Korea had a communist government with Kim Il-sung as the leader. He was supported by the communist Soviet Union.

South Korea formed a capitalist government with an elected president supported by the USA.

The two sides didn't like each other, and there were constant minor incidents along the border.

Timeline 1

In **1910**, Japan took control of Korea, which began a rule that would last for 35 years.

World War Two ended in **1945** with the surrender of Japan to the Allied Forces. The Soviet Union took control of the north, and the USA controlled the south. The Korean Peninsula was divided by the 38th Parallel.

By **1948**, the tension between the Soviet Union and the USA led to the Cold War. Korea was caught up in the Cold War conflict. North and South Korea became two separate countries as a result.

In **1950**, the Korean People's Army (KPA) of North Korea crossed the border and invaded South Korea. The United Nations denounced this, and troops were sent to the region to help South Korea.

Japanese Control of Korea

Koreans were forced to fight for Japan in World War Two

The Japanese Empire annexed Korea in 1910 and tried to destroy Korean culture in the years up to 1945.

The education system forbade the speaking of Korean in schools and universities as Japan tried to force Koreans to speak Japanese. Thousands of books were burned, and historical documents were destroyed in an attempt to wipe out Korean culture. Naturally, the Koreans fought back.

In this period, around 100,000 Japanese families settled in Korea, and approximately one million Koreans were forced to go and work in Japan.

The Japanese destroyed many historic buildings, and those that were not were turned into tourist attractions for wealthy Japanese visitors.

World War Two and the defeat of Japan did not mean independence for Korea. Although Japanese rule was ended, the peninsula was divided along the 38th Parallel. This division was intended to be short-term, but it became permanent because of the Cold War between the Soviet Union and the USA.

A communist ruler backed by the communist states of the Soviet Union and China was set up in the north. In the south, a capitalist government was supported by the USA and the newly formed United Nations.

The Start of the Korean War

Thousands of South Koreans flee from the advancing North Korean Army

On August 15, 1948, South Korea (the Republic of Korea) was established. Around one month later, the Democratic People's Republic of Korea (North Korea) was set up.

The border between North Korea and South Korea was artificial and had been drawn along the 38th Parallel. The North Korean leader, Kim Il-sung, wanted to invade the south and make Korea one communist state. In 1949, he asked the Soviet Union for help, but the Soviet leader, Joseph Stalin, refused.

Stalin didn't think that North Korea had the capabilities to launch such an attack and was concerned about what the USA and its allies would do.

Over the following 12 months, the Korean leader built up the military into a formidable force. When the Chinese sent back many battle-hardened Korean troops, and with Soviet equipment, the North had become far more powerful than the south.

North Korean forces in 1950 numbered between 150,000 and 200,000. They were organized into ten infantry divisions, a tank division, and a small air force. The North had 200 fighter planes and 300 tanks. The population of North Korea was just over 9 million people.

The population of South Korea was 20 million. The South had around 98,000 troops, no tanks, and just a few fighter planes.

On June 25, 1950, at dawn, North Korean troops crossed the 38th Parallel with a massive artillery bombardment as support. By June 28, North Korean troops had taken the capital of the south, Seoul.

The United Nations authorized military assistance for South Korea.

Timeline 2

On **September 12, 1950**, North Korean forces reached the 'Pusan Perimeter' in their advance through South Korea.

The North Korean troops were driven back, and on **September 25, 1950**, the South Korean capital, Seoul, was liberated.

In **October 1950**, the North Korean Army was pushed back into North Korea. When the United Nations (UN) forces got close to the Chinese border, Chinese troops entered North Korea and attacked. The UN forces retreated.

By **December 1950**, Chinese forces had succeeded in driving out American and UN forces from North Korea. However, the Chinese had lost many soldiers. It is estimated that around 80,000 had been killed or wounded.

The Pusan Perimeter

UN troops wait for another attack by the KPA

When the Korean People's Army (KPA) attacked Southern Korea, the United Nations sent troops to help the South Korean forces, who had not been able to stop the attack.

By June 28, 1950, the KPA had taken the capital of South Korea, Seoul.

The US forces sent to the Korean Peninsula could not halt the advance of the KPA and were forced further and further back.

South Korean, American, and British troops made a last stand in August in a defensive area called the Pusan Perimeter. This stretched for 140 miles around the port of Busan.

What was to unfold between August 4 and September 18, 1950, was the first major battle of the Korean War.

The South Korean, American, and British forces numbered 140,000.

The North Korean force (KPA) numbered 98,000.

After being constantly defeated by the KPA, the fight around Busan would be crucial.

The UN forces fought off repeated attacks for six weeks. The air superiority of the UN forces meant that the KPA had huge problems with supply lines.

A landing behind the KPA troops at Inchon caused the collapse of the North Korean resistance, and they retreated to the border.

UN Forces Attack North Korea

US tank crew take a break

With the South Korean capital, Seoul, back in the hands of the South Koreans and the North Koreans on their side of the border, it was decision time.

The idea to invade the north was approved, and on October 7, 1950, UN troops crossed the border.

On October 12, UN Forces captured the North Korean capital, Pyongyang, and moved towards the border with communist China. The situation had been reversed.

China acted quickly and sent 250,000 troops to help fight the UN Forces.

The ferocity of the attack by Chinese troops overwhelmed the UN troops, and they were forced back over the border after suffering heavy losses.

Timeline 3

On **January 4, 1951**, North Korean and Chinese troops recaptured Seoul.

On **March 14, 1951**, UN forces liberated Seoul from communist troops.

In **April 1951,** the American President, Harry S. Truman, relieved General MacArthur of the command in Korea. He put General Mathew Ridgeway in command.

Peace talks began on July 10, 1951, but the fighting continued.

The Chinese Attack South Korea

Fighting in the streets of Seoul

With the success of driving the United Nations troops out of North Korea, The Chinese leader, Mao Zedong, thought it was possible to take South Korea and unify the Korean peninsula.

The start of the Chinese offensive in January 1951 resulted in the Chinese taking the South Korean capital, Seoul. The Chinese saw that the resistance of the South Korean troops was the weak link in the United Nations Army, and they exploited it fully.

For the Americans, the advance of Chinese forces into South Korea was considered a disaster. The American military commander General MacArthur said that he thought the only way ahead was to defeat the Chinese by using America's nuclear weapons. The American President did not echo this opinion. However, the exhausted Chinese and North Korean forces ran out of steam and were eventually held by the UN forces. This revived the morale of UN troops.

In March 1951, there was a counteroffensive against the Chinese. This led to the recapture of Seoul, which had been devastated by the constant attacks from both sides.

Over one million people had populated the capital city of South Korea before the war, but in March 1951, this population had dwindled to less than 200,000. There was a lack of sanitation, medical supplies, and food and water. Many people were starving.

In the spring of 1951, the UN forces advanced a few miles into North Korea and prepared defensive lines as a buffer to stop the

Chinese from reinvading. This was done to stop Seoul from falling into enemy hands again.

In April 1951, a Chinese counter-attack aimed to break through the buffer zone and retake Seoul. The events around the Imjin River saw the Chinese advance held up by the British. The British were outnumbered by the Chinese but held on for three days before being forced to retreat.

The battle of Imjin River was one of the deadliest fought during the Korean War. The result enabled UN forces to withdraw to a stronger defensive position near Seoul, where the Chinese advance was eventually halted.

The fighting around the Imjin River was the last significant battle of the 'mobile phase' of the war in Korea. Both sides realized that a complete victory would be almost impossible to achieve.

Negotiations for a truce were started in July 1951 at Kaesong, but a deal was not reached until 1953.

While the negotiating teams from the two sides argued, the troops from both sides fought skirmishes to gain control of strategic areas. The fighting was done either in extreme cold or blistering heat. The idea behind most military operations from 1951 onwards was to improve the negotiating position for the impending truce.

General Douglas MacArthur

General MacArthur observes the troops landing at Inchon

When the communist troops from North Korea invaded South Korea in June 1950, Douglas MacArthur was given command of the US-led coalition of UN troops.

Under his command, the North Koreans were forced back over the border and then were pushed back to the Chinese border.

When the Chinese retaliated, MacArthur favored using nuclear bombs against them. The American President, Harry S. Truman, was worried that an attack would start World War Three and that the Soviet Union would get involved. Because of this, he refused to authorize an attack on the Chinese mainland.

President Truman realized in April 1951 that MacArthur was fully behind escalating the war in Korea rather than limiting it. He removed the general from command.

MacArthur returned to the USA in April 1951 and was welcomed back as a war hero. He publically criticized the policies of the president.

There were calls for him to run for president as the Republican candidate, but Dwight Eisenhower was chosen.

MacArthur died in 1964, aged 84.

The First Battle of Seoul

North Korean leader Kim Il-sung ordered the attack on the south

The battle took place between June 25 and June 28, 1950.

The North Korean forces crossed the 38th Parallel on June 25, 1950. There were troops supported by artillery and tanks.

The South Korean Army could not cope with the speed and ferocity of the attack. They had no tanks and no anti-tank weapons.

The South Korean forces retreated, and the North Korean Army occupied Seoul on the 28th of June.

As a result of the attack, the President of the USA, Harry S. Truman, promised to assist, and the United Nations Security Council (UNSC) passed Resolution 84. This resolution authorized assistance to South Korea.

South Korea had 65,000 troops

North Korea had 107, 0000 troops

South Korean losses included 44,000 missing, wounded, or dead.

North Korean losses were 1,112 Injured or dead

An emphatic victory for North Korea.

The Battle of Osan

The arrival of Task Force Smith in South Korea

The Battle of Osan took place on July 5, 1950, at Osan in South Korea.

This was the first time that American troops had come up against North Korean forces in the war.

An American task force named Task Force Smith arrived at Osan near Seoul, with orders to delay the North Korean advance until more US troops could arrive. The American task force lacked the anti-tank equipment needed to stop the North Koreans. The North Korean tanks swept through Task Force Smith and continued to advance.

The Americans then engaged with around 5,000 North Korean troops and were eventually overwhelmed.

The American task force retreated, having failed in its mission.

The US forces numbered 540 troops

The North Koreans had 36 tanks and 5,000 infantry

There were 60 Americans killed, 21 wounded, and 82 captured.

There were 42 North Koreans killed, 85 wounded, and one tank destroyed

This was a victory for North Korea

The Battle of Inchon (Incheon)

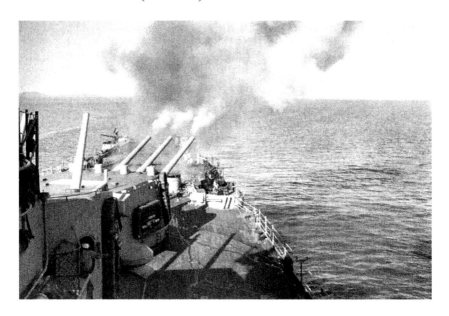

USS Toledo shells the shoreline before the troops land

The Battle of Inchon took place between September 10 and September 15, 1950.

The battle involved a UN force of troops and 261 naval ships.

The battle started on September 15 with the landing of UN troops from ships onto the beaches near the city of Incheon. There was a heavy naval bombardment that supported the landing.

This was a hazardous and daredevil attack masterminded by the American General, Douglas MacArthur.

The attack coincided with the breakout of UN forces from the Pusan Perimeter. The North Korean troops retreated with heavy losses.

Troops from the USA, UK, and Canada numbered 40,000

Soldiers from North Korea numbered 6,500

The UN lost 209 troops with 809 wounded

350 North Korean troops were killed

This was a victory for the United Nations and the South Koreans.

The Second Battle of Seoul

UN troops take back Seoul street by street

The Second Battle of Seoul happened in late September 1950 and resulted in the UN forces retaking the capital of South Korea.

After the UN troop landings at Inchon and the breakout of the Pusan Perimeter, the speed of the advance towards communist-held Seoul was slow.

The fighting was fierce, mainly because of the arrival of two crack-fighting units from the Korean People's Army (KPA). The KPA wanted to stall the UN offensive to allow Seoul to be reinforced and also for the withdrawal of troops from the south.

The retaking of the capital was essential to General MacArthur, even though he knew that concentrating on the city would allow thousands of North Korean troops to escape back to North Korea.

As UN troops entered Seoul, they were faced with formidable resistance. The North Koreans had built their defense positions well in the city, and at times, the fighting was from house to house.

Anxious to tell the world that Seoul had fallen, it was announced that Seoul had been liberated at 2 pm on September 25. In fact, it would take an additional two days for the fighting to stop.

The UN forces consisted of 40,000 troops from the USA, South Korea, the UK, and Canada.

The North Korean troops numbered 7,000.

About 400 UN troops were killed

Several thousand North Korean troops were either killed, wounded, or taken prisoner.

The battle was a victory for the UN.

The Battle of Ch'ongch'on River

This battle took place between November 25 and December 2, 1950.

The Chinese had entered the war when UN troops got too close to the China, North Korean border. They had succeeded in forcing the UN troops back towards South Korea. As a freezing winter closed in and the snow fell heavily, the Chinese attacked UN positions at Ch'ongch'on River.

The Chinese Army attacked UN forces in the Ch'ongch'on River valley on the night of November 25, 1950. Although the UN forces avoided being surrounded by the Chinese, they suffered heavy casualties and were forced to retreat.

The battle resulted in all UN forces retreating to the 38th Parallel.

The UN had 250,000 troops from the USA, South Korea, Turkey, and the United Kingdom.

The Chinese and North Korean troops numbered 230,000.

Around 11,000 UN troops were killed, wounded, or missing.

The Chinese and North Koreans had 10,000 battle casualties.

This was a decisive victory for China, which freed North Korea from UN forces.

The Battle of Chosin Reservoir

UN troops break through the Chinese lines

This battle took place around four weeks after the Chinese had entered the war. China's leader, Mao Zedong, had ordered his army commanders to destroy the United Nations forces. The fighting was fierce between November 27 and December 13, 1950. The snow made conditions extremely difficult.

The UN forces were taken completely by surprise by the Chinese attack. What followed for the next 17 days was a brutal battle in freezing conditions.

Around 30,000 UN troops were surrounded and attacked by 120,000 Chinese troops. Even though the UN troops were outnumbered, they were able to break through and retreat to the port of Hungnam. They inflicted heavy casualties on the Chinese troops.

The retreat of the UN troops after the Battle of Ch'ongch'on River and the evacuation from the port of Hungnam marked the complete withdrawal of UN troops from North Korea.

The UN force consisted of 30,000 US, UK, and South Korean troops, of which around 13,000 were killed, wounded, or missing.

There were an estimated 120,000 Chinese troops, of which an estimated 60,000 were killed or wounded.

The Third Battle of Seoul

This battle is also known as the Chinese New Year Offensive, and it came after the Chinese defeated UN forces at the Battle of Ch'ongch'on River.

After this defeat by the Chinese, the UN forces were at an all-time low, and it was contemplated leaving the Korean Peninsula.

On the orders of Chinese leader Mao Zedong, the Chinese Army crossed the 38th Parallel and headed for Seoul. This was an effort to force all foreign troops out of South Korea.

With the advance of Chinese troops, Seoul was evacuated on January 3, 1951.

The Chinese Army captured Seoul, but the attack had the opposite effect to what Mao Zedong had intended. Instead of demoralizing, the UN forces it stirred up support to defend South Korea.

The UN Army would soon go on the offensive, and the Chinese troops were exhausted after having fought their way into the capital.

The UN force numbered around 136,000 and was made up of soldiers from the USA, South Korea, the UK, Thailand, and Australia. There were about 800 casualties and deaths.

The Chinese Army had 170,000 soldiers. There were around 8,000 either killed or wounded.

Even though this was another victory for China and North Korea, tactically, it was a defeat because it reignited the United Nations into taking back South Korea.

Operation Ripper

UN air superiority played a big part in the Korean War

Operation Ripper is often called the fourth Battle of Seoul. It took place between March 7 and April 4, 1951.

Operation Ripper was designed to destroy as much of the Chinese Army as possible and retake Seoul and the 38th Parallel. Before the attack began, UN artillery bombarded the Chinese in the biggest artillery bombardment of the Korean War.

The city of Seoul was retaken for the final time and has not changed hands since. The objective of reaching the border between north and south was also achieved. What was not achieved was the destruction of the Chinese military capability. The Chinese troops managed to withdraw to North Korea and avoid being wiped out.

The United Nations forces that took part in the attack were from the USA, South Korea, UK, Australia, New Zealand, Philippines, and Canada.

This was a victory for the United Nations.

The Battle of Imjin River

Centurion tanks played a part in the battle of Imjin River

This battle took place between April 22 and April 25, 1951.

The Chinese Army attacked United Nations troops along the border in an attempt to break through and recapture Seoul. The UN forces had been very successful in the period January to March that year and had established a border beyond the 38th Parallel, in what was called the Kansas Line.

The position under attack was defended mainly by British troops, though there were also some troops from Belgium.

The UN forces were heavily outnumbered but held off the Chinese for three days before retreating. This is widely regarded as a heroic stand that ultimately gave other army units time to regroup and set up defenses.

Although this was considered a defeat, the action of British troops at Imjin River saved Seoul from falling into Chinese and North Korean hands.

This was one of the last skirmishes of the 'mobile war,' Both sides realized that to get 100 percent victory was impossible, so they built up defenses to stop the other side from invading.

Peace Talks

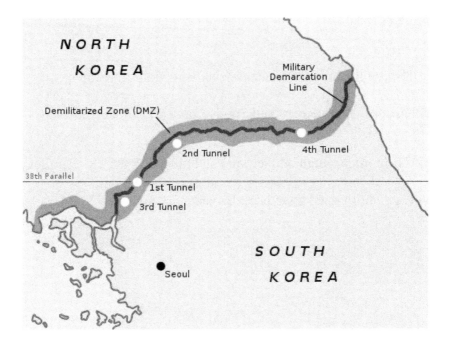

Peace negotiations started at Kaesong in North Korea. There were too many differences between the sides, and they broke down. They were relocated to Panmunjom and continued for a further two years.

One of the big problems was prisoners of war. Many North Koreans and Chinese did not want to be repatriated (sent home).

Hostilities between the two sides continued while the talks were being held.

Eventually, the Korean Armistice Agreement was signed on July 27, 1953.

The South Korean President never signed the agreement, so technically, North Korea and South Korea are still at war today.

The border remained the same and ran along the 38th Parallel, with a demilitarized zone on either side.

Korean War Trivia

Even though the Korean War ended on July 27, 1953, there are still 7,000 US soldiers classified as missing in action.

The war lasted less than three years, but many people died because of it. Around five million were dead, wounded, or missing, and around half were Korean civilians from both sides.

The war in Korea was the first military action (Proxy War) of the Cold War between the West and the Soviet Union.

There are many movies about the First World War and the Second World War, but very few about the (forgotten) Korean War. Some of the best are The Manchurian Candidate (1962), Pork Chop Hill (1959), and Birthday Boy (2004).

It is a weird fact that for people born since the war, South Koreans are on average about two inches taller than North Koreans.

Many countries sent troops to fight against North Korea. These were Sweden, Norway, and Italy (medical assistance only). Turkey, Thailand, South Africa, New Zealand, Luxembourg, Holland,

Greece, Britain, France, Ethiopia, Colombia, Canada, Belgium, Australia, and the USA.

One of the biggest dangers during the war was the weather. Many soldiers died before they saw any fighting as temperatures dropped during the harsh Korean winter. Temperatures were recorded in Korea as getting as low as -54 degrees Fahrenheit.

MASH (Mobile Army Surgical Hospital) units were used for the first time in this war. They were set up close to combat zones to enable more lives to be saved.

The TV series M*A*S*H was about a medical unit in the Korean War. It was on TV from 1972 until 1983. The final episode was the most-watched in TV history.

Pocket History

For more information about the Pocket History Series, visit the Amazon page

https://www.amazon.com/George-Joshua/e/B073BX9FYJ/ref=dp_byline_cont_ebooks_1 Click Follow, and you will get updates on new publications.

Other Books in the Pocket History Series

World War Two Facts and Trivia

Weird and Interesting War Facts

The Titanic Story

The American Revolutionary War

World War One Facts and Trivia

The Early American Colonies Explained

The Cold War Explained

Understanding the French Revolution

The UFO Riddle

The Ancient Sumerians for Children

The Korean War Explained for Children

The Human Body Explained for Children

Attributions

No machine-readable author provided. 아흔~commonswiki assumed (based on copyright claims)., CC BY-SA 3.0 <http://creativecommons.org/licenses/by-sa/3.0/>, via Wikimedia Commons

Map of the Korean Peninsula

Author and licence can be found here

https://commons.wikimedia.org/wiki/File:Map_of_the_Korean_Peninsula.png

Rishabh Tatiraju, CC BY-SA 3.0 <https://creativecommons.org/licenses/by-sa/3.0>, via Wikimedia Commons

Korea DMZ

Author and licence can be found here

https://commons.wikimedia.org/wiki/File:Korea_DMZ.svg

Printed in Great Britain
by Amazon